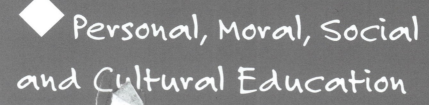

Personal, Moral, Social and Cultural Education

GROWING UP TODAY

Me as a citizen

Key Stage 2/P4–7

Carole Barnickle and Duncan Wilson

HOPSCOTCH
EDUCATIONAL PUBLISHING

◆ Contents

Published by Hopscotch Educational Publishing Company Ltd, 29 Waterloo Place, Leamington Spa CV32 5LA 01926 744227

© 2000 Hopscotch Educational Publishing

Written by Carole Barnickle and Duncan Wilson
Design by Steve Williams
Illustrated by Cathy Gilligan
Cover illustration by Cathy Gilligan
Printed by Clintplan, Southam

Carole Barnickle and Duncan Wilson hereby assert their moral right to be identified as the authors of this work in accordance with the Copyright, Designs and Patents Act, 1988.

ISBN 1-902239-46-6

Every effort has been made to trace the owners of copyright of poems in this book and the publisher apologises for any inadvertent ommissions. Any persons claiming copyright for any material should contact the pubisher who will be happy to pay the permissions fees requested and who will amend the information in this book on any subsequent reprint.

◇ ◆ ◇ ◆ ◇ ◆ ◇ ◆ ◇ ◆ ◇ ◆ ◇ ◆ ◇ ◆ ◇ ◆ ◇ ◆ ◇ ◆ ◇ ◆ ◇ ◆ ◇

This book is one of a set of four books, each looking at a different area of the DfEE's recommendations for the teaching of PSHE and Citizenship at Key Stage Two. In these books we are trying to share ideas with colleagues. We hope you will find something that you are able to use in your school.

We work at a three-form entry Junior School in Bournville, Birmingham. We have been actively involved in promoting citizenship throughout our school for the past four years.

Many of you may be wondering:
◆ what citizenship is
◆ how you can fit citizenship into an already overcrowded timetable
◆ what activities you can use to promote citizenship in your school

We think that citizenship in schools is about giving children the skills to become responsible individuals and independent thinkers. They should be able to make informed judgments that will enhance their quality of life and that of others, while, at all times, showing respect for themselves and other people, irrespective of gender, culture, religion and ethnicity.

While we realise that this is quite a challenge we feel that these are important skills that have long been neglected and can be taught across the curriculum. Although these lessons stand alone, we feel that they also lend themselves to the Literacy Hour or as part of an RE scheme of work.

In our school, circle time is well established as part of the weekly timetable. For colleagues not familiar with circle time, the concept was first developed by Jenny Mosley (see 'Quality Circle Time' published by Learning Development Aids). Jenny developed the concept to help schools effect individual and

organisational change. The aim is to empower everyone in the school community to have an equal voice in the discussion, recognition or game being used through the use of various strategies.

In our school it is a time of the week when the classroom becomes much less formal, allowing the teacher and children the opportunity to get to know one another, develop team building skills, play co-operation games and present and discuss views.

We have a very active School Council made up of representatives from each class. We are also involved with the local Development Education Centre. Our school Debating Society discusses issues raised by the children and many of our children have had the opportunity to attend debates at the Council House. Our assemblies reflect citizenship issues.

For a school to be successful in its delivery of the citizenship curriculum it has to have a whole-school approach to the subject. We feel very strongly that it is not a subject that can be taught once a week, but that it should be reflected in the whole ethos of the school and in the attitudes expressed by the pupils and staff. We feel that the development of these attitudes among the children is the key to monitoring the success of your citizenship programme.

Where do you begin?
Circle time
Our school began by introducing circle time into the timetable, using this as a means for the children to raise and discuss their worries and concerns surrounding such issues as bullying, friendship groups and name calling, in a non-threatening environment. We found that it was also a useful tool for helping Year 3 children get over the transfer from Infant to Junior School.

◇ ◆ ◇ ◆ ◇ ◆ ◇ ◆ ◇ ◆ ◇ ◆ ◇ ◆ ◇ ◆ ◇ ◆ ◇ ◆ ◇ ◆ ◇ ◆ ◇ ◆ ◇ ◆ ◇ ◆ ◇

Rules are established at the beginning of the session. Generally there are three rules, the first being that a person only speaks when they are holding the magic object (we have a dinosaur egg teddy which turns inside out into a baby dinosaur), the second being that everyone else must listen when another person is talking and the third being that if someone does not want to speak they are not pressured to and can 'pass' their turn on to the next. It is up to you whether or not you add further rules to specific discussions. For example, if discussing the issue of bullying it might be reasonable to set the rule that no-one can use any names.

You will see that in many of the chapters we have recommended that the children are to be seated as for circle time. Given the constraints of many classrooms, it is up to you to decide how it would work best for you. Circle time sessions can be run with the class and teacher seated in a circle on the floor, with the class at their desks or with the children facing you sitting down.

The School Council

Our School Council was started in order to give the children a voice, allowing them to raise any concerns they had about their time in school with the two teacher representatives who also sit on the Council. It has proved to be a very effective way for children to communicate with teachers and vice versa. We have undertaken projects in school and the community that have been suggested, organised and run by the Council representatives. The Council meets once a fortnight for half an hour during lunch and the children have gradually taken on the roles of chairperson and secretary. Council representatives are elected by the class and are changed each year.

We have noticed that children sitting on the Council have become more confident and articulate because they have been elected by their classmates to present the views of their class to the Council. If children in our classes have concerns, we encourage them to put these concerns to their representative, who will then raise and discuss them at the next meeting.

Circle time and a School Council are two ways that you can start to challenge the attitudes of the children and staff in your school. We also hope that using the ideas in this book will make a difference.

Using this book

The chapters are all set out in the same way. Each begins with a focus for the chapter, which contains the learning objectives taken from the 'National Curriculum Framework for PSHE and Citizenship'.

These are followed by key points and notes for teachers detailing our thoughts about the concepts being taught. We have tried to anticipate and discuss some of the problems colleagues might have and, as practising teachers, we have suggested strategies that we have used to help us deliver the material with sensitivity.

After this are two lesson plans, one each for younger and older children. By younger children we mean Years 3 and 4 and by older children we mean Years 5 and 6. Each lesson plan follows the format of a whole-class introductiory session, suggestions for group work followed by a plenary session and includes two differentiated photocopiable worksheets.

Several chapters also give details of generic sheets and these are to be found at the back of the book. At the end of each chapter are suggestions for further activities that could be undertaken relating to the chapter focus.

We have not suggested a time schedule for the lessons, but you could adopt a three-part format of introduction, development and plenary. We recommend that each lesson should last approximately one hour. Many of the lessons lend themselves to more than one session and could be developed over several weeks.

About each chapter

Chapter 1: Me and my opinions

◆ The children will become more aware of their opinions and will begin to develop the confidence to express them. They will learn where to research their opinions and how to present them. They will be encouraged to look at the media and pressure groups and will begin to evaluate the opinions expressed by these agencies with their own.

Chapter 2: Me and my responsibilities

◆ The children will become aware of the purpose and meaning of rules. They will recognise that there are different sets of rules for different places and situations. They will participate in the process of making positive rules for their classroom.

Chapter 3: Me and my behaviour

◆ The children will begin to develop an awareness of what constitutes inappropriate behaviour and the situations in which this can arise. They will rehearse justifying and presenting a viewpoint to an individual, small group and the whole class.

Chapter 4: Me and my decisions

◆ The children will begin to understand why conflicts arise. They will begin to consider that there are two sides to every argument and that the solution will not necessarily suit both sides. They will begin to recognise that there are several ways to resolve a disagreement.

Chapter 5: Me and my identity

◆ Younger children will produce a character study for another child in the class. They will consider their own identity and will be given the opportunity to compare it with another. They will begin to realise that we are all individuals with our own unique identities.

◆ Older children will develop an appreciation of the religious diversity of the society in which they live. They will begin to recognise that these religions share many common themes.

Chapter 6: Me and democracy

◆ Younger children will be introduced to the concept of democracy. They will relate this to the everyday situations they may find themselves in.

◆ Older children will begin to develop an understanding of the processes of democracy and the institutions that support it at local level. They will consider the practicalities of policy making. They will prepare, rehearse and deliver a short manifesto. They will develop an understanding of the voting system.

◆Me and my opinions

Focus

◆ In preparing to play an active role as citizens, pupils should be taught:
2a: to research, discuss and debate topical issues and problems and events
2k: to explore how the media present information.

Key issue: What are my opinions and where do I get them from?

◆ Many people, especially children, are not comfortable with the idea of talking in front of others. Sometimes a child will remain quiet, feeling nervous of what others will think of their ideas and opinions. They can feel that their ideas are not as valid as those expressed by other children who may just be more extrovert. These children can be overlooked by adults. They should be encouraged to develop strategies to help them express themselves in front of others.

◆ All children should be encouraged to discuss the media and recognise the extent to which it can influence their ideas and opinions.

Notes for teachers

We live in a country in which we are allowed to vote and express ourselves freely. These freedoms are also responsibilities and children need to appreciate this.

Reserved children present a particular challenge to teachers. We have to encourage them to reach a specific level for the Speaking and Listening strand of English, a strand which they find the greatest challenge of all. While listening to adults and other children tends to be something that comes naturally, speaking in response is altogether different. We have all known children whose Speaking and Listening level has been well below their other levels in English. In addition, it is just as important for their personal development and self esteem that they are taught these skills so they can put forward their own desires, opinions and ideas.

At the other end of the spectrum, we also have a duty to ensure that the children who have the confidence to speak in front of others take time to consider what it is that they want to say and that they say it in a responsible manner that is inoffensive to others. An opinion said loudly, and sometimes aggressively, does not make it any more valid than an opinion held personally.

While we are encouraging children to develop their own individual opinions and preferences, we should give them the opportunity to assess these against the stereotypical views sometimes portrayed in the modern media.

The children should become aware of issues such as:
◆ subliminal advertising strategies
◆ how the media can try to influence the public
◆ how important the television and media are in shaping attitudes and values
◆ the need to challenge the way in which some information is presented
◆ the subtlety used by advertising companies in the marketing of products
◆ the impact of photographs
◆ respect for and awareness of the different ethnicities that make up today's multi-cultural society.

◆ Me and my opinions

Intended outcomes

◆ The children will become more aware of their opinions and will begin to develop the confidence to express them.

◆ They will learn where they can research their opinions and how to present them.

◆ They will be encouraged to look at the media and pressure groups and begin to compare opinions expressed by these agencies with their own.

Resources

◆ a copy of Jack and the Beanstalk

◆ the photocopiable activity sheets on pages 8 and 9

Children who have not begun to develop an understanding of alternative points of view would benefit from doing the following activity before the lesson. Ask them to write a report about an incident in the playground with one person taking one viewpoint and another taking an opposing viewpoint. Is it always easy to decide who is right or wrong? If this happens in low level situations in the playground, can they begin to understand that it might also happen at a national level in the press?

Lesson plan for younger children

Introduction
◆ Ask the children to vote on who the baddie is in Jack and the Beanstalk. (Try this cold, as during the lesson the children will have cause to rethink.)
◆ Then, tell/read the story. Are they able to retell the story to the teacher? Establish that they understand the following points. Who is the baddie in the story? Why are they the baddie? What have they done? Why is the Giant cross with Jack? Why is Jack afraid of the Giant? Is he right to be cross with the Giant? What do you think you would have done if you were the Giant or Jack?

Group activities
Explain to the children that they are going to work in groups or pairs to consider the relative rights and wrongs of the actions of both Jack and the Giant.

Photocopiable activity sheet 1
This sheet is for lower achievers. They should consider questions that analyse the situation, such as 'Who was the baddie in the story?', 'What did he/she/they do that was naughty?' and 'Was it fair that they got the blame?'. They then create the 'Wanted' posters for the Giant and for Jack including a description and what it is they have done to be wanted by the Fairy Tale Police.

Photocopiable activity sheet 2
The higher achievers work in pairs to produce two letters to the Chief of Police. In one, they defend the actions of Jack and in the other the actions of the Giant.

Plenary session
Selected children can share their work. Then the class could discuss which of the characters they feel to be the guilty party. Are either of them totally innocent or totally guilty? Then ask the children to vote again on who they consider to be the baddie. If the vote remains the same or changes, discuss this with them. Can they think of any situations they have been involved in where the outcome has been more complicated than they thought it would be? Can they see that there might have been more than one point of view involved in resolving that situation?

Questions to ask
◆ Is there always a right version of events or will there always be disagreements?
◆ Are the correct versions of events always the most popular?
◆ Is there ever a totally correct version of events?
◆ Are fairy tales always fair to the villains/heroes? Is that fair?
◆ Have you ever read or heard about anything that you didn't think was fair?

◆ Jack and the Giant ◆

◆ Think about Jack and the Giant in the story 'Jack and the Beanstalk'. The Giant has always been seen as the baddie and Jack as the goodie. But is that true?

◆ Think about what Jack did. Was he naughty in any way? Think about why he went up the beanstalk. Had he been invited? What happened in the Giant's house? Who was naughty first? Is it fair that the Giant got all the blame?

◆ Complete these wanted posters for Jack and the Giant.

WANTED	WANTED
Jack is wanted because he	The Giant is wanted because he
_____	_____
_____	_____
_____	_____
_____	_____

◆ Who do you think is the baddie – Jack or the Giant? Why?

_____

_____

_____

Hopscotch ◆ Me as a citizen

◆ Jack and the Giant ◆

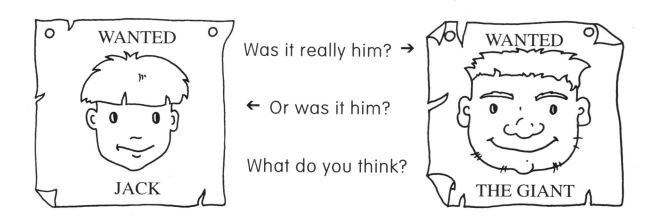

◆ In the story 'Jack and the Beanstalk', the Giant has always been cast as the baddie and Jack as the hero. But is this really fair?

◆ Think of reasons why both Jack and the Giant may have been falsely represented. Write them around the pictures.

◆ Now work with a friend to write two letters to the Chief of Police. One of you should pretend to be Jack and the other the Giant. In your letters explain why you feel you were not to blame for anything that happened in the story.

◇ ◆ ◇ ◆ ◇ ◆ ◇ ◆ ◇ ◆ ◇ ◆ ◇ ◆ ◇ ◆ ◇ ◆ ◇ ◆ ◇ ◆ ◇ ◆ ◇ ◆ ◇ ◆ ◇ ◆ ◇ ◆ ◇

Intended outcomes

- The children will become more aware of their opinions and will begin to develop the confidence to express them.
- They will learn where to research their opinions and how to present them.
- They will be encouraged to look at the media and pressure groups and begin to compare opinions expressed by these agencies with their own.

Resources

- a recent newspaper
- the same news story from several different newspapers
- the photocopiable activity sheets on pages 11 and 12
- the generic sheet on page 54

Lesson plan for older children

Introduction

- Discuss with the children something they have seen or read in the news that has interested them. Have they all heard about this story? Read a suitable article from a recent newspaper to the class and discuss how each of the sides involved might feel. For example, they could discuss the latest sports scandal looking at whether or not a sports person's right to privacy is outweighed by our right to know what they have been up to.

Questions to ask

- Can the children identify both points of view?
- Can they identify where the points of view diverge?
- Can they relate their own views to this discussion?
- Can they make a decision about which point of view they feel is the stronger?
- Can they see that there are two conflicting points of view and that they are both equally valid?

Group activities

Explain to the children that they are going to complete an activity where they will look in greater depth at the newspapers. Tell them that by the end of the session you will have expected them to have formed opinions about why articles are presented in certain ways and to have considered how important the layout and presentation of the article are to the content. Encourage them to consider how writers try to convince readers that their recount of the event is the correct one.

Photocopiable activity sheet 1

Give the lower achievers a selection of newspapers that contain the same piece of news. Ask them to read the different stories and then complete the chart on the activity sheet showing which details are the same and which are different. They should think about why there are differences between the two reports.

Photocopiable activity sheet 2

Give the higher achievers an article concentrating on one side of a topical issue of interest or use the one provided on page 54. They should then use the activity sheet to produce an article that takes the opposite point of view. Let them discuss the opposing points of view with each other before completing the sheet.

Plenary session

Some of the children can share their work. Discuss the relative strengths of the arguments. Are either of them completely right or completely wrong? Can the children appreciate that without knowing both sides of the argument, they are not in any true position to form an opinion on a subject.

Questions to ask

- Have both sides of the argument been presented? Are they both valid?
- Do we really need to hear both sides of the argument?
- If we think it is right, why does it matter what other people think?
- When you next read an article what will you look for?

◆ Same or different? ◆

◆ You have been given several different newspapers which report the same story. With a friend, read the different reports and underline any important facts or details. Look at the headlines and the layout of the stories. Are they the same in each paper? Complete the chart below to help you to recognise what is the same in all the papers and what is different.

The article is about _____ _____ _____	The page number that the story is on	How much space the story has been given	The main focus of the story	Number of pictures accompanying the story
Paper 1 _____				
Paper 2 _____				
Paper 3 _____				

Which newspaper did you prefer? _____

Why? _____

Do you think that newspapers always report news in a fair way? _____
Why do you think this is? Write your ideas on the back of this sheet.

◇ ◆ ◇ ◆ ◇ ◆ ◇ ◆ ◇ ◆ ◇ ◆ ◇ ◆ ◇ ◆ ◇ ◆ ◇ ◆ ◇ ◆ ◇ ◆ ◇ ◆ ◇ ◆ ◇ ◆ ◇ ◆ ◇

◆ What do you think? ◆

◆ Your teacher has given you a newspaper article that gives one side of an argument. You may or may not agree with the views given. Your task is to write an article that gives an opposite point of view.

◆ Before you begin writing, share your ideas with a friend. Make notes to help you to write your article. Think of a good headline.

PHOTOCOPIABLE PAGE

Further activities to develop understanding

◆ Show the children a range of advertisements which they should discuss and try to decide what product they are advertising. Can they decide why the advertising companies have used the images/music/actors that they have to sell the products? What is the advert teaching us about the type of person who buys/uses this product?

◆ Look at the visual information on a cereal box and discuss who the product is aimed at. What are the differences in packaging, presentation, marketing ploys and ingredients between cereals aimed at an adult market and at a children's market? The children should begin to challenge the way these products are portrayed by the advertising companies.

◆ Ask the children to look at a favourite book, picture or painting and write about/discuss with someone else why they like it. Is it because they have read something about it, know something about it or just have a personal preference for it?

◆ Look through the press, collecting all the information found on Africa. What impression of Africa do these images leave the children with? Collect their ideas. Do they really believe Africa is as it is presented in the press?

◆ Collect examples of the magazines read by the children. What do they think of them? What are their favourite parts? Why? What bits of the magazine don't they like and why?

◆ From a bank of topics the children could select a topic which they then research and present to the class in one of a variety of ways. They could prepare a talk to give to the class; they could make a poster containing all the relevant information; they could record their talk as a radio/video documentary. Encourage them to use reference library materials, the Internet, papers, 'experts' and specialist agencies.

◆ Discuss with the children what issues concern them at a school/local/national/global level. At a school level this could be covered through the use of a School Council. At a local level, invite a local councillor to talk to the children and answer their questions. At a national level the children could video conference with MPs and with children in schools in other parts of the country. At a global level the children could e-mail and use video conferencing links to share views with other parts of the world. We appreciate that not all schools have access to these resources but, if they do, this would certainly be a good opportunity to develop this.

◆Me and my responsibilities

Focus

◆ Preparing to play an active role as citizens, pupils should be taught:
2b) why and how rules and laws are made and enforced, why different rules are needed in different situations and how to take part in making and changing rules
2d) that there are different kinds of responsibilities, rights and duties at home, at school and in the community, and that these can sometimes conflict with each other.

Key issue: Why do we need to think about our rules, responsibilities and rights?

◆ Everybody is better at doing some things than others. We should help children to think about what abilities they have and to recognise their strengths.
◆ They should be encouraged to think about and respect the strengths and weaknesses of their friends and classmates.
◆ When weaknesses have been identified they should be encouraged to discuss how these might be addressed.
◆ Children should be encouraged to explore their own feelings about other people in order to investigate how these people might in turn feel about them.

Notes for teachers

It is important that children become reflective adults, able to take responsibility for themselves and their behaviour. They must recognise that, as individuals in our society, they are born with certain rights. They must recognise that their rights can be protected by the laws and rules of the society in which they live.

Taking responsibility for ourselves and our behaviour is one of the milestones that we must pass to become responsible citizens. We must encourage children to take responsibility for areas of their lives as early as possible.

Adults will accept certain standards of behaviour from a two-year-old child, that they would not accept from a ten-year-old. We assume that the ten-year-old has a greater level of personal responsibility for his or her own behaviour. We must encourage children to recognise when their behaviour is inappropriate, why it is inappropriate and the consequences of that misbehaviour.

We want our children to be able to reflect back on their behaviour and recognise the effect that it has on others. Part of this process is learning to respect their own rights and those of other people. We all have the right to be fed and clothed, to be kept in a secure and safe environment, to be listened to, to voice our opinions, not to live in fear of any physical, sexual or verbal abuse and to be educated.

We want our children to know not only when their rights are being violated by the actions or behaviour of others, but also when their actions are violating the rights of someone else. If the bully's victim lives in fear of persistent verbal or physical abuse, then his or her rights are being violated. Both the victim and the bully need to be aware of this.

In our society we would like to think that the rules and laws we live by ensure that the individual rights of each person are protected and respected. In some other societies around the world, rules and laws can be used to oppress the rights of the individual. It is important that the children are aware of this and are encouraged to value their rights and the values of the society they live in.

Lesson plan for younger children

Introduction

◆ Write the word 'rules' on the board and ask the children to consider a classroom/ school/home/road with no rules. Record some of their thoughts on the board. Then discuss what rules mean and why we have them. Encourage them to recognise that we have rules to try to make people feel safe, happy and secure. This is because rules prevent inappropriate behaviour and actions that could result in people being unhappy, unsafe and insecure.

◆ Discuss the rules that the children are aware of. Write them on another part of the board under headings: Rules at Home, Rules at School and Rules Elsewhere. Encourage them to recognise that there are different rules according to where we are. Are there some rules that we always have to live by?

Group activities

Group the children in mixed ability groupings of two or four (according to your situation). Give each group a copy of the generic sheet on page 55 which contains rules, some of which are reasonable and others unreasonable. Ask them to underline reasonable rules in one colour and unreasonable rules in another. Then choose one reasonable rule and one unreasonable rule and justify their decision.

Photocopiable activity sheet 1

This sheet is more suitable for lower achievers. They are required to complete a set of rules, using the words provided.

Photocopiable activity sheet 2

This is more advanced. No words are provided but the children are given some advice on writing their rules.

Plenary session

Collate the rules generated by the children on the board. For rules that begin 'Do not', lead a discussion converting these rules from negative to positive, in order to reinforce positive behaviour. For example, convert 'We don't run in the classroom.' to 'We always behave sensibly when we are in the classroom'. In this way you will put together a set of positive rules. For incidences of misbehaviour in the future, you can then say 'Well these are your rules you are breaking. We all agreed.'

Questions to ask

◆ What would a school without rules be like?
◆ What is the purpose of having rules?
◆ What rules do you know?
◆ What rules do you have at home/at school/while walking along the playground?
◆ What rules would you like in your classroom?
◆ What rules are appropriate/inappropriate?
◆ Do you know any rules that are silly?
◆ What do you think is the most important rule you have at school/at home/on the road?

Intended outcomes

◆ The children will become aware of the purpose and meaning of rules. They will recognise that there are different sets of rules for different places and situations. They will participate in the process of making positive rules for their classroom.

Resources

◆ felt-tipped pens
◆ a set of prepared rules, some reasonable, some unreasonable
◆ the photocopiable sheets on pages 16 and 17
◆ the generic sheet on page 55

◆ Classroom rules ◆

◆ In the space below write five good rules for your classroom. Use the words in the box to help you.

FIVE GOOD RULES for my class
by _____

◆ _____

◆ _____

◆ _____

◆ _____

◆ _____

nice	caring	look after	working	helping
good	behaviour		always	never

◆ Classroom rules ◆

◆ In the space below write five good rules for your classroom.

Here are some tips to help you.

Try to be positive. Begin by saying 'We always…' rather than 'Don't…'

Try to make your rules relevant to everyone in your class.

Make sure your rules are realistic and fair.

FIVE GOOD RULES for my class

by _____

◆ _____

◆ _____

◆ _____

◆ _____

◆ _____

◆ Now think about what sanctions there should be for people who don't keep the rules.

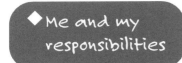
Me and my responsibilities

Intended outcomes

◆ The children will become aware of the purpose and meaning of rules. They will recognise that there are different sets of rules for different places and situations. They will participate in the process of making positive rules for their classroom.

Resources

◆ pencils and crayons
◆ the generic sheets on pages 56 and 57
◆ the photocopiable activity sheets on pages 19 and 20

Lesson plan for older children

Introduction

◆ Discuss what a punishment is and why people are punished. What do the children consider is a fair punishment and what is not? Ask them to tell you things they have been in trouble for. You may need to be tactful here.

Group activities

Organise the class into groups and give each group a copy of the generic sheet on page 56. The groups should discuss things they have been in trouble for, decide how serious they were, then write them on the sheet in the relevant places, for example something serious that they knew they would be in big trouble for (red light), something that they thought they might get into trouble for, but weren't too sure (yellow light) and something they got into trouble for, but didn't think they deserved to (green light). They do not have to put their names on the sheet. Give them a few minutes to complete this then share their traffic lights and write some of them on the board. When several have been written up, discuss as a class whether or not they felt that the punishments they received were fair. Then, still in their groups, ask them to complete the photocopiable activity sheets.

Photocopiable activity sheet 1

This contains pictures of various misdemeanours that might take place at home, at school and in the street. The children should write two statements for each saying what punishment or otherwise they would expect for this misdemeanour and what punishment they think they deserve.

Photocopiable activity sheet 2

This sheet is for higher achievers. They are asked to look at an illustration (the generic sheet on page 57) which shows some developing situations taking place inside and outside a local shop. The children should circle any potential trouble and then on the activity sheet write brief descriptions of the trouble spots identified and the consequences of those actions.

Plenary session

Discuss with the children whether or not it is fair that people are punished. Are they able to recognise the need to be responsible for their own actions? Discuss the purpose and nature of the punishment. Do they feel that the punishment fits the crime?

Questions to ask
◆ Why do we need rules?
◆ Can you think of bodies that have rules?
◆ Who makes the rules?
◆ Who gives, or how do people/groups get the power to make/enforce the rules?
◆ Are all rules fair?
◆ Are all rules fair to everyone?
◆ Why?/Why not?

◆ Trouble, trouble, trouble ◆

◆ Look at the pictures. Can you see what has happened?
For each one complete the two sentences.

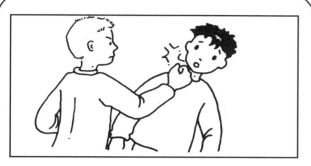

If I did this, this would happen to me

_____

_____

If I did this, this should happen to me

_____

_____

If I did this, this would happen to me

_____

_____

If I did this, this should happen to me

_____

_____

If I did this, this would happen to me

_____

_____

If I did this, this should happen to me

_____

_____

If I did this, this would happen to me

_____

_____

If I did this, this should happen to me

_____

_____

◆ Someone's in trouble ◆

◆ Look at the 'Trouble spots' picture. As you can see, there are a number of situations developing. Draw a coloured circle around all the 'trouble spots'. Choose three of the situations and in the boxes below describe what is happening and what you think the consequences will be.

PHOTOCOPIABLE PAGE

Further activities to develop understanding

◆ Ask the children to write about 'The naughtiest thing I ever did and what happened to me'.

◆ Are the rules that we live by different from the rules our parents and grandparents lived by? How have they changed and why? Invite a parent or grandparent in to school to talk about them.

◆ Ask the children to complete a group brainstorming activity considering who makes the decisions at school, at home, in their community, in the city and in the country. What decisions do the children have individual, independent control over on a day-to-day basis? What decisions are they able to have some influence over? Why is this the case?

◆ Ask the children to do a piece of writing or a poem entitled 'If only I hadn't', regretting moments of bad behaviour.

◆ Where else do the children encounter rules? Discuss any religious rules that they might know about or live by. What similarities are there between the sets of rules established by the world's major religions?

◆ Do some research or diary-type writing with accompanying pictures on 'How I look after my pet'.

◆ What rights are the children aware they have? Are these rights shared by people throughout society or are some people more privileged than others?

◆ What happens when people break the rules established by their society or religion? What is the purpose of punishment: deterrent, pure punishment or reform?

◆ Ask the children to discuss and then write about the people who help them to become responsible and how they help them do this.

◆Me and my behaviour

◆ Preparing to play an active role as citizens, pupils should be taught:
2c) to realise the consequences of anti-social and aggressive behaviours, such as bullying and racism, on individuals and communities
2e) to reflect on spiritual, moral, social and cultural issues, using imagination to understand other people's experiences.

Key issue: What are the consequences of my behaviour? How does my culture affect the way I behave?

◆ All children must be taught how to behave.
◆ Teachers, parents and the media are becoming increasingly concerned with the behaviour of children.
◆ The number of children with behaviour disorders is on the increase in British schools.

Notes for teachers

Children with behaviour disorders represent a significant challenge in the classroom. Teachers are finding more and more that they need to help these children learn how to:

◆ socialise
◆ share
◆ co-operate
◆ cope with frustrations
◆ attempt basic learning tasks

Unfortunately, statistics in many LEAs demonstrate that the number of these children in our schools is on the increase. There are many reasons why this may be so, including the changing nature of the society they live in and the diverse nature of the lifestyles they lead. As teachers, it is becoming a larger part of our job to attempt to remedy this growing problem.

We must learn to separate the difficulty from the person. It is the inappropriate behaviour that is bad, not the child who behaves in this manner. We must learn to value the children in our care and teach them how to value each other and themselves.

Children behave inappropriately for many reasons. While we accept that many children misbehave because they are going through a learning process during which they they must differentiate between what constitutes acceptable and unacceptable behaviour, others misbehave for different reasons. They may be suffering from a medically recognised condition or they may be reacting against personal problems at home or school.

As teachers we should look for the root cause behind the misbehaviour and then develop the appropriate strategies to implement a behaviour recovery programme.

All children should be taught how to behave if they are to play a meaningful, purposeful and productive role within society. They should start to learn from an early age what is and isn't acceptable.

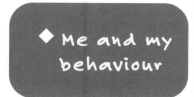

◆ Me and my behaviour

Intended outcomes

◆ The children will begin to develop an awareness of what constitutes inappropriate behaviour and the situations in which this can arise. They will rehearse justifying and presenting a viewpoint to an individual, small group and the whole class.

Resources

◆ the generic sheet containing Ben's story on pages 58 and 59
◆ the photocopiable sheets on pages 24 and 25
◆ scissors

Lesson plan for younger children

Introduction

◆ Introduce the lesson with the story Ben's Day (pages 58 and 59). The story details a day in the life of a junior school child where the child breaks many rules, ranging from the innocuous to the serious. At each stage the respective adults allow the child to get away with it. Use this story as the focus for discussion during the introductory session.

◆ Ask the children what they notice about the child in the story? They should answer that he breaks lots of rules. Discuss which rules have been broken. Do all the class agree that the rules have been broken?
(Be aware that these questions may result in children raising difficult issues regarding punishments at home.)

Group activities

Organise the children into ability groups and explain that they are going to try to put a series of six misdemeanours in order of seriousness.

Photocopiable activity sheet 1

This sheet requires the children to discuss, cut out and order the misdemeanours from naughtiest to least naughty. The descriptions are quite brief and the language level more suitable for lower ability children. The children should discuss and compare their list with that of the child sitting next to them, trying to agree an order of naughtiness. The pairs then share and discuss their lists with others in the group and produce an agreed order for the group.

Photocopiable activity sheet 2

This sheet contains the same misdemeanours as those on Activity sheet 1 but the descriptions are written in more detail using more advanced language. The sheet is more suitable for children with higher abilities. Again, they should discuss and compare their list with that of the child sitting next to them, trying to agree an order of naughtiness. The pairs then share and discuss their lists with others in the group and produce an agreed order for the group.

Plenary session

One child should act as speaker for each group and present their findings to the class. The class should discuss the lists produced, giving suggestions about why they consider one misdemeanour to be worse than another. Is there agreement over which misdemeanour is the most/least serious?

◆ How naughty? ◆

◆ Some people can be naughty. Read the sentences below. Then cut them out and put them into a new list. Put the naughtiest thing at the top and then the next.

◆ When you have sorted them into a list, share them with a friend. Is your friend's list the same as yours? If not, work together to make another list that you both think is right.

Tom wouldn't do his work. He was talking.

Sam hit Jack back.

Amy wouldn't eat her supper. She did not like cabbage.

Laura wouldn't tidy her bedroom. She was playing.

The children took the chocolate from the shop.

Tom took an apple but he didn't ask his mum first.

◆ How naughty? ◆

◆ Read through the misdemeanors below. Then cut them out and put them in order from naughtiest to least naughty.

◆ When you have done this, look at the person's next to you. Have they put them in the same order as you? Together, talk about the misdemeanors and put them into a new list that you both agree with.

◆ Now compare this new list with the other children in your group. Your task is to make one list that that you all agree with. Decide who will be the one to report back to the rest of the class.

Tom was told to stop talking and get on with his work three times in ten minutes.

Sam hit Jack because Jack had hit him during morning playtime.

Amy hated cabbage. When she was given it for supper she refused to eat it.

Laura's mum asked her to tidy her bedroom but she carried on playing.

The children went to the shop to buy chocolate. They didn't have enough money to pay so they just took the chocolate and ran.

Tom took an apple from the kitchen without asking his mum for permission.

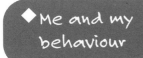

◆ Me and my behaviour

Intended outcomes

◆ The children will begin to develop an awareness of what constitutes inappropriate behaviour and the situations in which this can arise. They will rehearse justifying and presenting a viewpoint to an individual, small group and the whole class.

Resources

◆ the generic sheets containing poems on pages 60 and 61, and the generic sheet containing a playground picture on page 62
◆ the photocopiable activity sheets on pages 27 and 28

Lesson plan for older children

Introduction
◆ As a stimulus to the lesson discuss "Bully" by Pauline Stewart or "Left Out" by Celia Warren (see page 60 and 61). Ask questions to begin your discussion.

Questions to ask
◆ Who do the children think wrote the poem?
◆ How do we think the person who wrote the poem felt? What tells us this?
◆ Why did the person feel this way?
◆ If you were the bully, how would you feel to read this poem?
◆ Why was the person in the poem bullied?
◆ Why did the poet write the poem?

◆ Record answers to these questions on the board in note form. Seat the children as for a circle time activity and give small groups a copy of the generic sheet containing a playground scene picture on page 62. Discuss with them what is happening in the picture and how the people might feel. The boy is injured and the girl is pointing to a group of boys who are playing football. What is she suggesting? Can they see any evidence of bullying? The boy in the background looks as though he might be about to push the boy in front of him. Tell the children they are now going into groups to do a similar task using photocopiable activity sheets.

Group activities
Photocopiable activity sheet 1
This activity sheet shows three scenarios in which something is happening with regard to children's behaviour. This is a lower ability activity where the children have to write about what is happening in the pictures but they have a box of words to help them.

Photocopiable activity sheet 2
This activity sheet shows the same three scenarios as on Activity sheet 1. These children have not only to write about what is happening but also about what they think of the behaviour. They are not given the help of a word box.

Plenary session
Discuss the pictures with the class. Are the children able to say whether the pictures show something innocent happening or might there have been some bad behaviour going on? Do any of the pictures imply bullying? Then discuss how bullies should be treated when they are caught. Do the class think they should be punished or counselled? Do they consider that one of a bully's problems is that they are unable to see what harm and upset they are causing their victims?

◆ What is going on? ◆

◆ Look at these pictures. Write what is happening in each one. Use the words in the box below to help you.

_____
_____
_____
_____
_____

_____
_____
_____
_____
_____

_____
_____
_____
_____
_____

accident	behaviour	argument	challenge	injury
steal	taking	talking	shouting	

◆ What is going on? ◆

◆ Look at these pictures. What do you think may have caused what you see happening? Do you think anyone is behaving badly? Put your thoughts in writing alongside each picture. Include what you think are the causes and what you think of the behaviour. Continue on the back of this sheet if you need more room.

◇ ◆ ◇ ◆ ◇ ◆ ◇ ◆ ◇ ◆ ◇ ◆ ◇ ◆ ◇ ◆ ◇ ◆ ◇ ◆ ◇ ◆ ◇ ◆ ◇ ◆ ◇ ◆ ◇ ◆ ◇

PHOTOCOPIABLE PAGE   **Hopscotch** ◆ Me as a citizen

Further activities to develop understanding

◆ The following topics can be the subject of class debate or discussion in pairs or small groups. Be careful that what people say does not cause offence.

What do people in the class do that you don't like? What do people do at home that you don't like? Do you know if you have ever done something that other people don't like? How does this make you feel? How do you think this makes other people feel? What happens to other people when they behave in this way? What happened to you when you behaved like this?

◆ Can the children identify anti-social behaviour from newspaper pictures and predict what will happen next?

◆ Ask the children to consider what it means to be happy about yourself and feel in control of your life?

◆ Discuss the following: What is bullying? What do you think you should do if you know someone is being bullied? What should you do if you are being bullied? What do you think you should do if you are a bully? How do you think the bully and the victim feel? Investigate through role play, circle time and through a discussion of relevant poems.

◆ Ask the children to draw a picture of what they think a bully looks like. They should complete speech bubbles showing the things that a bully might say. Around the outside of the picture they could write down what the bully might do. The plenary session should discuss the nature of bullying as being something physical or mental that is repeatedly carried out against a person by another person or group of people.

◆ Ask the children to rank a selection of misdemeanours typical of children of their age group that occur at school or at home. They should explain why they think one misdemeanour is more serious than another.

◆Me and my decisions

Focus

◆ Preparing to play an active role as a citizen, pupils should be taught:
2f) to resolve differences by looking at alternatives, making decisions and explaining choices.

Key issue: How can I resolve differences and what decisions am I allowed to make?

Notes for teachers

In an ideal world we would like everybody to be able to:

◆ listen openly and honestly to other people's opinions
◆ recognise and accept that other people have different opinions to our own
◆ recognise when and when not to put our point of view into a discussion
◆ accept and admit when we are in the wrong
◆ talk rather than shout at other people
◆ use discussion rather than physical means to resolve an argument
◆ think carefully before we make a personal comment about someone.

While we recognise that none of us can claim to have all these characteristics, it is important that children are challenged to think about how they speak to and treat other people. They should be made aware of how their actions or the way they express their opinions and feelings can affect other children and adults.

Part of this process is by learning through their own experiences in the playground and at home. For example, they learn about what upsets them or what they do that upsets others. This can also be reinforced and taught in the classroom. They need to discuss and be made aware of issues around resolving differences and making decisions.

As adults we lead by example. Children observe and learn from the way adults interact with each other. Children learn to mimic adult behaviour from an early age. As a result, adults should treat children as they would expect children to treat others.

When children do misbehave, we must make sure we explain to them that certain standards are unacceptable and the reasons why this is so. We should challenge our children to empathise with those whose feelings they have hurt and allow them to question their actions.

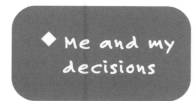

Intended outcomes

◆ The children will begin to understand why conflicts arise. They will begin to consider that there are two sides to every argument and that the solution will not necessarily suit both sides. They will begin to recognise that there are several ways to resolve a disagreement.

Resources

◆ the photocopiable sheets on pages 32 and 33

Lesson plan for younger children

This is a very open ended lesson which could be used to discuss a number of issues relevant to the children. If a child's main concern is with their friends or if a child is being bullied either physically or mentally, then these concerns can be brought up and discussed during the lesson in a non-threatening situation. The children should make the decision about what it is they want to raise and discuss.

Introduction

◆ Set a scenario for the children to discuss. This could be "Have you ever been in a situation when…" These situations might include times when they have been upset by other people or when they have upset other people. This is an opportunity to bring incidents that may have happened recently into the discussion. The children should be encouraged not to use the names of the people involved. The emphasis of the lesson is on resolving differences and not merely rehashing them.

Group activities

Tell the children that they are going to work in pairs (make these pairs mixed ability), with one child acting as a scribe. They are going to write down conversations between children that have resulted in incidents where one of the parties has become upset.

Photocopiable activity sheet 1

The children should complete the top part of the sheet then underline what was said that caused the original upset. When they have completed this, tell them to discuss what might have been done or said to resolve the situation. These could include fetching an adult, walking away, thinking carefully about what has been said and replying accordingly – anything that they think would diffuse the situation that is brewing. (Try not to put strategies into the their minds at this stage as these strategies and others will be discussed during the plenary session.) They should then rewrite the same dialogue on the lower half of the sheet, this time including the strategy they have chosen to resolve the conflict.

Photocopiable activity sheet 2

This activity is similar to that on Activity sheet 1 but the children are required to do more detailed writing. They should also consider what might have been said to resolve the situation then write the story again, this time including the strategy to resolve the conflict.

Plenary session

As a class share some of the pairs' original and revised dialogues. Write some of the strategies identified on the board and discuss the effectiveness of each, considering the consequences of what is done. If they suggest fetching an adult, they should also consider what the adult might say to resolve the situation. Agree strategies that are likely to help the situation and those that are likely to make the situation worse.

◇ ◆ ◇ ◆ ◇ ◆ ◇ ◆ ◇ ◆ ◇ ◆ ◇ ◆ ◇ ◆ ◇ ◆ ◇ ◆ ◇ ◆ ◇ ◆ ◇ ◆ ◇ ◆ ◇ ◆ ◇ ◆ ◇ ◆ ◇

◆ The argument ◆

◆ Sam and Rashid have argued about whose turn it is to be in goal. In the speech bubbles, write an angry conversation that left Sam upset.

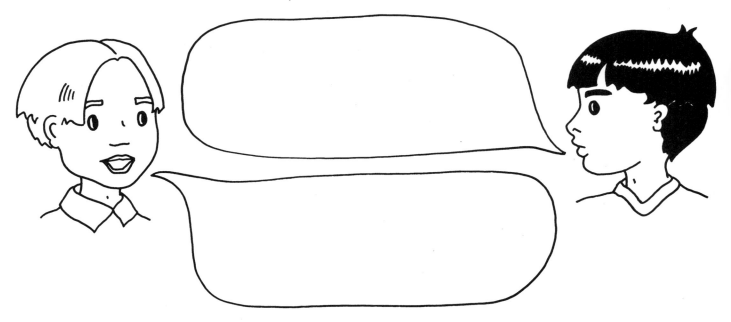

◆ Now rewrite the conversation so that neither of them become upset.

PHOTOCOPIABLE PAGE

◆ The argument ◆

This is Clare

This is Becky

This is Dalvinder

◆ Clare, Becky and Dalvinder can be good friends but they can sometimes argue. Write down a conversation that could have made them fall out.

_____

_____

_____

_____

_____

◆ Now write the conversation again, this time making sure the girls stay friends.

_____

_____

_____

_____

_____

Intended outcomes

◆ The children will begin to understand why conflicts arise. They will begin to consider that there are two sides to every argument and that the solution will not necessarily suit both sides. They will begin to recognise that there are several ways to resolve a disagreement.

Resources

◆ the photocopiable activity sheets on pages 35 and 36

Lesson plan for older children

This lesson could also be undertaken with younger children and could be extended into two or three lessons. For additional lessons refocus the children with circle time games (see Introduction) and reflect back on previous discussions.

Introduction

◆ Set up a circle time activity. Ask the children to talk about recent incidents at school that have resulted in arguments that have upset them or other people. This could have been in the current term or week, but they should not start looking too far back into the past! Establish as a rule that no names are to be used at all during the discussion.

Group activities
Photocopiable activity sheets 1 and 2

Put the children into two circle groups and give one group copies of Activity sheet 1 and the other copies of Activity sheet 2. Ask them to consider what is happening in their picture as it is passed around the circle. If the discussion in either group needs to be advanced, ask questions such as:

◆ What has happened just before this picture?
◆ Who are the people in the picture?
◆ What will happen next?
◆ What would you like to see happen next?
◆ Why would you like to see this happen next?
◆ How could this incident be resolved?
◆ What could have happened to stop this incident taking place?

Plenary session

When the discussions have ended, bring the children back into one circle and refocus them on their own and their friends' experiences which had been discussed at the start of the lesson. Ask how their incidents were handled and whether or not they were sorted out satisfactorily. If they feel that they were not sorted out satisfactorily, what do they feel might have been done to have resolved the situation? What could they have done to have prevented the situation occurring in the first place?

◆ What's it all about? ◆

◆ What's it all about? ◆

Hopscotch ◆ Me as a citizen

Further activities to develop understanding

◆ Ask the children to think about all the decisions they have made in the last day/week. Why did they make the decisions they made? What did they consider before they made the decision? Was the decision based on taste, safety or another reason?

◆ Ask the children to consider when they decide to cross the road. What do they have to think about before they make the decision to step into the road? What could happen if they did not go through these thought processes before stepping out?

◆ What decisions have been made for them in the last day/week? Who decided what time they went to bed, what time they got up, what they ate for dinner?

◆ The children could consider situations in which they have fallen out with others at school or at home then consider how these situations were resolved. What was done to make the resolution satisfactory? What happened that made the resolution unsatisfactory? What could we do to resolve differences ourselves?

◆ Ask the children to discuss the word "Sorry". Is it just a word that gets them out of trouble or is it a part of the decision making progress that children take on the road to improving their behaviour?

◆ Ask the children to think about some of the things they did yesterday and write them down. They should then write alongside each who made the decision: them, someone at home, their teacher or someone else. At the bottom of the sheet they could write why these people made these decisions.

◆ Ask the children to consider a bad decision they made during the last week. They should think about the consequences of making that decision and about what might have happened had they not made it. They could then investigate whether any other decisions were made as a consequence of the first one. Were they good or bad? They could draw a decision tree with 'yes' or 'no' options and a possible plan of events for each of these answers given, until they reach a conclusion for the paths taken.

◇ ◆ ◇ ◆ ◇ ◆ ◇ ◆ ◇ ◆ ◇ ◆ **Further activities to develop understanding** ◆ ◇ ◆ ◇ ◆ ◇ ◆ ◇ ◆ ◇ ◆ ◇

◆Me and my identity

Focus

◆ Preparing to play an active role as citizens, pupils should be taught:
2i) to appreciate the range of national, regional, religious and ethnic identities within the United Kingdom.

Key issue: Who am I and what do I believe?

◆ Children's personalities develop rapidly.
◆ Children learn about themselves by making decisions and expressing material, ethical, moral and constitutional preferences.
◆ Children should investigate and express their beliefs and personality.

Notes for teachers

By encountering and coping with experiences and situations at home and at school, children learn about themselves and their personalities every day. They quickly learn about material things that they like and dislike, such as foods, games and toys, and will show a preference from a very early age.

As they grow older they will be faced with making decisions on emotional, constitutional, ethical and moral issues that will affect themselves, their family, friends and community. These decisions should reflect the personality and beliefs of the child. Children should be allowed to express themselves and their beliefs honestly and openly and feel safe and secure while doing so.

At the same time, they must be taught how to do this in a sensitive and informed manner. We have all known children who have commented loudly on the bus statements such as 'That man's got a big nose', oblivious to the fact that 'that man' is probably fully aware of this fact and probably isn't too keen for it to be broadcast quite so openly. We must teach children when and where it is appropriate for them to voice their opinions and the difference between holding an opinion and being openly rude.

In this chapter, the children will have the opportunity to investigate and express their beliefs and opinions and present them to others.

◆ Me and my identity

Intended outcomes

◆ The children will produce a character study for another child in the class. They will consider their own identity and will be given the opportunity to compare it with another. They will begin to realise that we are all individuals with our own unique identities.

Resources

◆ the photocopiable activity sheets on pages 40 and 41

Lesson plan for younger children

Introduction

◆ Brainstorm the word 'identity' and then lead a discussion about the meaning, collecting ideas on the board. Tell the children that a person's identity is not just what they look like, but what they like to do, to eat, to play, what their religious beliefs are, what sort of person they are, how they treat others, how they behave, the customs they adopt and so on.

◆ Explain that now they are going to look more closely at their own identities.

Group activities
Photocopiable activity sheet 1
This is for lower ability children to complete. They should be organised into pairs and then each draw a picture of their partner and complete a range of sentences around the picture.

Photocopiable activity sheet 2
More able children can complete the sheets in pairs, interviewing their partner. They should write on the sheet details about their partner's identity. The questions relate to looks, personality, religion and beliefs. These will help them to build up a picture of their partner's identity.

Plenary session
Play 'Guess Who?'. Read out some of the children's completed sheets and ask the class to discuss and decide who the description is of.

◆ Who are you? ◆

This is a picture of

_____

_____ has _____ hair.

_____ has _____ eyes.

_____ is _____ years old. _____ birthday is _____.

_____ likes _____ and _____.

_____ doesn't like _____ and _____.

_____ is special because

_____

_____

_____

_____

I found out these things about _____ family

_____

_____

_____

_____

◇ ◆ ◇ ◆ ◇ ◆ ◇ ◆ ◇ ◆ ◇ ◆ ◇ ◆ ◇ ◆ ◇ ◆ ◇ ◆ ◇ ◆ ◇ ◆ ◇ ◆ ◇ ◆ ◇

PHOTOCOPIABLE PAGE   **Hopscotch** ◆ Me as a citizen

◆ Who are you? ◆

This is a picture of

_____

Write 3 things that your friend likes.
◆
◆
◆

Write 3 things that your friend doesn't like.
◆
◆
◆

What makes your friend angry?
◆
◆
◆

What makes your friend sad?
◆
◆
◆

What makes your friend happy?
◆
◆
◆

Ask your friend these questions. They may not want to answer – you must respect that.

◆ What is your religion?

◆ What special events do you celebrate?

What two things make your friend special?
◆
◆

◆ Use these facts to write a description of your friend on the back of this sheet.

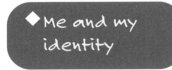
◆ Me and my identity

Intended outcomes

◆ The children will develop an appreciation of the religious diversity of the society in which they live. They will begin to recognise that these religions share many common themes.

Resources

◆ reference books detailing the religions Sikhism, Islam, Christianity, Buddhism, Judaism and Hinduism
◆ CD-Roms
◆ the photocopiable activity sheets on pages 43 and 44

Lesson plan for older children

Preparation
You will need to provide the children with a range of reference books or CD-Roms containing information about the religions Judaism, Buddhism, Hinduism, Sikhism, Islam and Christianity. This lesson looks at the diversity of religious beliefs in this country, while emphasising the themes common to them all.

Introduction
◆ Many different cultural, religious and ethnic groups live in harmony in our society today. They all help to make our country a diverse and interesting place. Tell the children that they are going to learn more about some of the religious groups that there are in our country. Brainstorm the main religions that exist in Britain today: Buddhism, Christianity, Islam, Sikhism, Hinduism and Judaism.
◆ Do the children know anything about the traditions of any of the religions listed? Write these on the board, discussing them as they are raised and emphasise common features. For example, each religion has an important text or texts; each religion gives guidance as to how to live a good life taking care of others in our society; each religion has its own important symbols and special days and each religion has an important figurehead.

Group activities
Tell the class that they are going to use a variety of sources of information to produce a piece of work about a religion they are unfamiliar with.

Photocopiable activity sheet 1
Lower ability children can work in pairs to complete this activity sheet. It asks them to unscramble the names of the six main religions and to find and list four 'Did you know?' facts for their chosen religion.

Photocopiable activity sheet 2
This asks higher ability children to collect a range of information about their chosen religion from reference books and other sources of information. They should draw and name the relevant symbols, festivals, texts and clothes.

Plenary session
Share and discuss the work produced and give the children the opportunity to raise their own personal experiences. Collect the information produced and display it around the classroom. Talk about how religion might be important to them. What do they think about religion? Why can religion be important to people? How can religion help people?

◆ Religions ◆

◆ Below are the names of the six major religions in the United Kingdom. Unscramble the letters to find out what they are.

<u>a</u> i <u>J</u> s <u>d</u> <u>u</u> m
J _____

<u>a</u> <u>l</u> s <u>m</u> <u>l</u>
I _____

<u>C</u> i <u>r</u> s <u>t</u> <u>a</u> i <u>t</u> i <u>h</u> n <u>y</u>
C _____

<u>d</u> <u>d</u> <u>B</u> <u>u</u> i <u>h</u> <u>m</u> <u>s</u>
B _____

i <u>h</u> k <u>S</u> i <u>s</u> m
S _____

<u>u</u> i <u>H</u> i <u>s</u> n <u>m</u> d
H _____

◆ Choose one of the religions and see what you can find out about it. Complete the sentences below.

Did you know _____

_____ ?

Did you know _____

_____ ?

Did you know _____

_____ ?

Did you know _____

_____ ?

◆ Religions ◆

◆ These are the six main religions in the United Kingdom – Buddhism, Christianity, Hinduism, Judaism, Islam and Sikhism. Choose one of them to investigate further, using reference books.

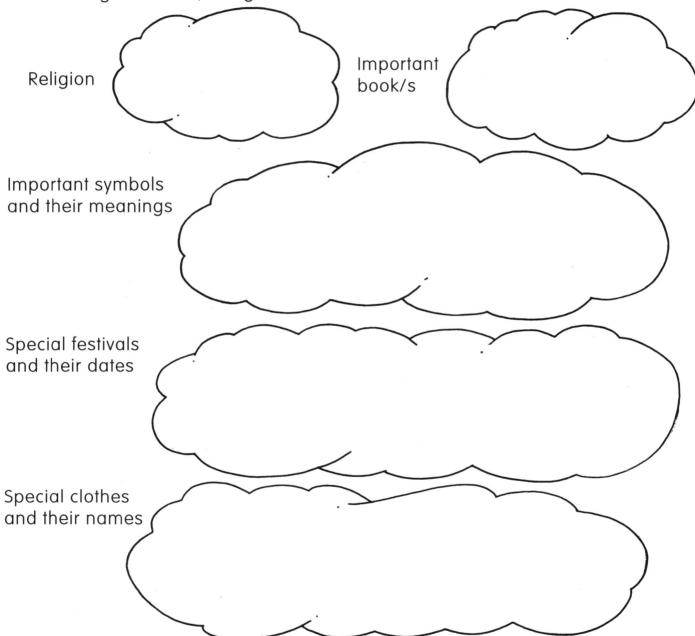

Religion

Important book/s

Important symbols and their meanings

Special festivals and their dates

Special clothes and their names

◆ When you have finished, think about other religions that share these features and the names they have for their special book, symbols, festivals and clothing. On the back of this sheet, write down your thoughts on how religion helps people .

PHOTOCOPIABLE PAGE

Further activities to develop understanding

◆ Discuss with the children who has been the biggest influence on their life. Can they remember who taught them how to read and write or the difference between right and wrong. Can they write down what the difference between right and wrong is? Discuss the meaning of having a conscience.

◆ Discuss with the children what they believe in. Are there things that they believe in for which there is no definitive proof? Can they explain why they still maintain their belief?

◆ In a circle time activity, let the children share who they are with each other. They should each ask their neighbour for information, such as favourite hobbies, books, films and so on, which will then be presented to the rest of the class.

◆ Discuss and share any rituals and customs that are observed at home. Make connections between the similar customs that are observed by the world's largest religions.

◆ Prepare a list of questions to ask an older member of the family and ask them to come in to the school to demonstrate the customs they grew up with. Discuss with the class why they feel the customs have changed. Is everybody happy that they have changed? Was there such a thing as the "Good Old Days"? Can each generation in a family remember how they altered the customs they had grown up with? How did their family react to that?

◆ Ask the children to consider what their strengths and weaknesses are.

◆ Discuss with the children who they find it difficult to get on with and why.

◆ How do they deal with situations they find difficult? Do they deal with them in the way they think they should?

◆ Can the children recognise and acknowledge what situations make them happy or sad. Why do they think they feel this way? Can they recognise and acknowledge situations where they make other people feel happy or sad?

◆ Give the children a story and ask them to consider how it makes them feel. Can they decide why it makes them feel this way?

◆Me and democracy

Focus

◆ Preparing to play an active role as citizens, pupils should be taught:
2g) what democracy is, and about the basic institutions that support it locally and nationally
2h) to recognise the role of voluntary, community and pressure groups.

Key issue: What is democracy and how can I be a part of the democratic process?

◆ The children must learn that it is the opinion of the majority that decides what is done.
◆ There are organisations at a local, national and global level that will allow the children access to the democratic process.

Notes for teachers

It is important that children are taught to understand and value the concept of democracy. In a democratic society, such as ours, people have the right to vote for the politician or political party whose policies they feel are most representative of their own views. The politician or party with the most votes then forms the governing body of the country.

Article 19 from the Universal Declaration of Human Rights[1], states that:

'Everyone has the right to freedom of opinion and expression; this right includes the freedom to hold opinions without interference and to seek, receive and impart information and ideas through any media regardless of frontiers.'

Our system of democracy is underpinned by the Universal Declaration of Human Rights which protects the rights of all people, including children, to form, hold and voice an opinion without fear of retribution from others.

We take democracy and human rights in our country for granted, often forgetting that historically many people have fought to protect and defend its principles. We forget that many people around the world do not enjoy the same privileges.

Children should be encouraged to realise the responsibilities that come with a democratic system. From an early age, they should be encouraged to think about wider issues that affect themselves and their community. They should be made aware of the institutions that serve the needs of their community initially at a local level and, as they grow older, at a national level. They must also learn how to access these institutions and to evaluate the roles they play in our society.

[1] Article 2 from the Universal Declaration of Human Rights, United Nations//Mango-Album Dada Co. Publication 1997 ISBN 92-1-100760-7

◆ Me and democracy

Intended outcomes

◆ The children will be introduced to the concept of democracy. They will relate the concept of democracy to everyday situations that they may find themselves in.

Resources

◆ the photocopiable sheets on pages 48 and 49

Lesson plan for younger children

Introduction

◆ As a class, discuss the term 'democracy'. Ask them to suggest a definition that is agreed by the majority of the class (you may need to guide this discussion to a successful outcome).

◆ Bring up for discussion the way the children play in the playground. Can they say who decides the game that is to be played by a group of friends? Is it an individual or a group decision? Ask them to consider the difference between the two.

◆ They should consider whether or not the most dominant child in a group is the one who makes all the decisions or whether the group comes to a joint decision.

◆ Ask them to consider why some groups allow the most dominant child to make all the decisions.

Group activities
The photocopiable activity sheets

Organise the children into small mixed-ability groups. Cut up the scenarios on the two photocopiable sheets, give each group one of the scenarios and ask them to dramatise the situation, considering a range of outcomes. They should develop and rehearse the situations to present to the class at the end of the lesson. One person from each group should be nominated by the rest of the group to present and explain each of the scenarios.

Plenary session

Each group should perform their scenario for the class. As a class, discuss what has taken place in each dramatisation. Can they decide whether or not the person who makes the decision makes it for themselves or for the group. Is the decision democratic?

◆ Democracy scenarios ◆

The children always played football with Tom. It was his ball and Tom always picked the teams and made up the rules. But one day …

Gemma, Pavinda and Sarah always played together but Gemma always decided which games they played. Until one day …

Ahmed, Yusuf and John were in the same class. Yusuf liked to be the boss when they worked together. He always did the writing, he always reported back to the class. Ahmed and John were fed up of this so…

 Hopscotch ◆ Me as a citizen

◆ Democracy scenarios ◆

Dalvinder was always in trouble. So were her friends. One day Dalvinder wanted to go to the local shop and steal sweets. She had worked it all out. Bobby was to create a diversion while Carl and Sonia stole the sweets. Bobby really did not want to go but he knew the others would get him if he didn't. What can he do?

A class of children have been asked to decide where to go on a school trip. Some children want to go to the zoo – they like larger animals. Ekena and Mary think it would be a great idea for the class to go to the local park and clear up all the rubbish. Ryan and Rory want to go to the adventure park where they have big rides. How will they decide?

Siobhan, Paul and Jeung-Eun were always falling out. Paul always wanted to play with Jeung-Eun and exclude Siobhan. Jeung-Eun wanted them all to play together. It made her sad when they argued. She liked them both. What can she do?

◆ Me and democracy

Intended outcomes

◆ The children will begin to develop an understanding of the processes of democracy and the institutions that support it at a local level.
◆ They will consider the practicalities of policy-making.
◆ They will prepare, rehearse and deliver a short manifesto.
◆ They will develop an understanding of the voting system.

Resources

◆ the generic sheets on pages 63 and 64
◆ the photocopiable activity sheets on pages 51 and 52

Lesson plan for older children

Introduction

◆ Tell the class that, in order for a party to be elected to Government, they must first let the people of the country know what they would do when they are in power. Each idea is called a policy and when policies are put together they become a manifesto. Each party must consider very carefully the practicalities of their manifesto, as, once elected, the voters will expect them to adopt their policies.
◆ Point out that some ideas are just impractical. For example, it is impractical for a party to promise free bikes for all children as a means of combating traffic congestion because the money wouldn't be available for such a scheme.
◆ Make sure that all the children can see copies of the generic sheets on pages 63 and 64. One sheet is ridiculous and impractical, the other more practical and realistic. Discuss these and encourage them to realise how the policies differ and to reach a decision as to whether or not the implementation of the policies would be practical and subsequently benefit society.

Group activities

Photocopiable activity sheet 1

This sheet is intended for lower ability children. On each side of the sheet is someone with a speech bubble stating that person's point of view. There are a range of subjects covered. The children should consider which of the two they would vote for and why.

Photocopiable activity sheet 2

This sheet is for more able children who are to write a manifesto for an imaginary politician. They should consider what they would like to do, how they would pay for their plans and who will benefit from their policies, should they be elected. These points will then be converted into a short speech which will be delivered to the class during the plenary session.

Plenary session

Ask some of the children to share their work with the class. Those who have completed Activity sheet 1 could explain their choices and give their reasons. Select three of the children who have completed Activity sheet 2 to come out and give their speech. The class should then discuss and evaluate each candidate before voting. When the voting has been completed, lead a discussion with the class about institutions that support democracy locally and nationally, such as local council departments, members of parliament and the media.

◆ Vote for me ◆

◆ Tick the boxes you agree with.

◆ On the back of this sheet, write some sentences to explain why you chose as you did.

◆ Vote for me ◆

◆ Write a short manifesto for an imaginary politician. You must consider how you are going to pay for your plans and who is going to benefit from your policies if you are elected.

If you vote for me I will

● _____

_____

● _____

_____

● _____

_____

● _____

_____

◆ Now think about the speech you will give to the voters. Write it out here. Continue on the back if you need more space.

_____

_____

_____

_____

_____

_____

PHOTOCOPIABLE PAGE

Further activities to develop understanding

◆ Discuss with the children the groups that run the school. Discuss the concept of accountability. What does it mean and who are they accountable to? Can they think of any other groups that operate voluntarily in the school? (School Council and PTA) What is the function of these groups? How are the groups formed, are they elected or chosen? When do they meet and what do they do?

◆ Are there groups that operate outside the school that the children participate in, such as Cubs, Scouts, Brownies or sports teams? How are these groups run? Who are these people accountable to? What is the purpose of these groups?

◆ How is the country run? Are the children aware of the Government, of the Houses of Parliament, of the different roles of the Queen and the Prime Minister, of the process of local and national elections? Do the children know who the local MP or councillor is for their area?

◆ The children could hold a class election to vote for a representative to the School Council (see Introduction). They could also hold a mock election.

◆ What groups are the children members of? Why have they joined these groups? What are they hoping to achieve through their membership? Why did they want to join these groups? The children could write letters to groups putting forward their point of view.

The children should be made aware of:
◆ groups at a domestic, local, city-wide, national and global level
◆ the purpose of groups at domestic, local, city-wide, national and global level
◆ the selection/election of groups at domestic, local, city-wide, national and global level
◆ the workings of groups at domestic, local, city-wide, national and global level.

◆ The children could undertake research topics into countries that do not have a democratic system of government. They could also research people in history who have fought to protect democratic principles.

◆ On a sheet of paper the children could write the name of an organisation they are familiar with (this could be their own school). Around this they should write down all the groups they can think of that affect the running of that organisation. Around these groups they should then write down what role each of these groups plays in the running of that organisation.

◆ An argument ◆

Today's children do not play enough sport. Sport and exercise are important for lots of reasons. Doctors say that the heart must be exercised when young in order for it to develop and grow properly. Sport helps to keep a child's brain active and lively because it represents a challenge that the child must think through.

Children learn about teamwork, co-operation, communication and the importance of rules when they take part in sporting activities. Instead of getting involved with sport, children these days watch four hours of television each day and play computer games. These activities are often done alone, so children do not learn how to talk to other people. They are also done sitting down so no physical activity is done at all.

If our national teams are to start to do better, today's children must spend less time watching television and playing on the computer, and more time playing sport.

PHOTOCOPIABLE PAGE

◆ Rules ◆

All my rules are good!

◆ Look at the list of rules below. Underline in blue the rules that you think are unreasonable. Underline in red the rules that you think are reasonable.

It's all right for you!

You must obey these rules at all times

- ◆ We always look after our property and the property of others.
- ◆ We always do our best work at home and at school.
- ◆ We always sit and work in silence during every lesson.
- ◆ We always go out into the playground at 10.45am every day in all weathers.
- ◆ We are never allowed to go out to play before we have finished all of our work.
- ◆ If we have a day off sick we must come to school on Saturday.
- ◆ We must wear our school uniform at all times.
- ◆ We must always make sure that we never deliberately hurt anyone.
- ◆ All children with blue eyes must sit at the back of the classroom.
- ◆ All people who are short sighted must sit at the front of the classroom.

◆ Now try to make a set of rules for your own class that are reasonable.

◇ ◆ ◇ ◆ ◇ ◆ ◇ ◆ ◇ ◆ ◇ ◆ ◇ ◆ ◇ ◆ ◇ ◆ ◇ ◆ ◇ ◆ ◇ ◆ ◇ ◆ ◇ ◆ ◇ ◆ ◇

◆ Trouble, trouble ◆

◆ Think about times when you have been in trouble.

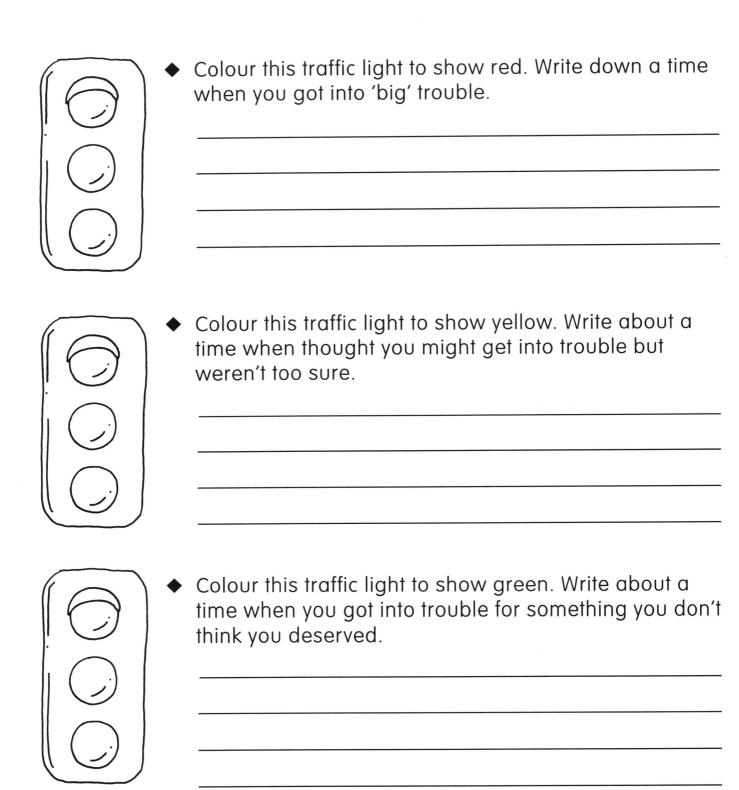

◆ Colour this traffic light to show red. Write down a time when you got into 'big' trouble.

_____

_____

_____

_____

◆ Colour this traffic light to show yellow. Write about a time when thought you might get into trouble but weren't too sure.

_____

_____

_____

_____

◆ Colour this traffic light to show green. Write about a time when you got into trouble for something you don't think you deserved.

_____

_____

_____

_____

 Hopscotch ◆ Me as a citizen

Trouble spots ◆

◆ Ben's story ◆

Mum opened the curtains and turned to Ben. "Come on Ben, time to get up!" she said. She went out of the room, looking over her shoulder as she went. Ben began to get out of bed, but as soon as his mum left the room he pulled the covers up under his chin and closed his eyes. "Ben, Ben are you up?" bellowed his mum up the stairs.

Ben said, "Just coming, I'm nearly ready". He sighed, why did he have to go to school? Why did he have to leave his nice warm bed?

"Ben, Ben hurry up!" came a cross voice from downstairs. "Your breakfast has been on the table for ten minutes."

Ben got out of bed and quickly got dressed. He went into the bathroom and put his toothbrush under the cold tap. He wet the flannel that his mum had put out for him and flung it into the sink. He crumpled up the towel and threw it to the floor.

"There you are!" said his mum. "Hurry up. Did you have a wash and clean your teeth?"

"Of course I did, Mum, I always do!" replied Ben, as he sat down to eat his eggs. If there was one thing Ben hated more than getting out of bed in the morning it was eggs. He waited for his mum to go out of the room and he scraped his plate into the kitchen bin. He opened the biscuit tin and grabbed a handful of chocolate biscuits and slipped them into his pocket. As soon as his mum dropped him off at school he would have his real breakfast.

Ben sat at his desk looking around the room. The other children were taking their homework out of their bags. Ben needed to think fast. Last night when he should have been doing his homework he had been out playing football. He had told his mum that the teacher had forgotten to give them any.

Ben put up his hand. "Sorry, Miss, but my brother ripped up my book. My mum said she would give me a letter but my Gran was ill and she had to take her to the hospital."

"Never mind Ben," said his teacher, "bring it in when you can. I hope your Gran gets better soon."

Ben smiled to himself and pretended to read his book.

At break time, Ben ran out of the classroom into the playground. All he could think about was playing football. He ran straight into a little girl and they both ended on the floor. Ben knew he would have to act quickly. This wasn't the first time he had caused an accident by running inside school which he knew was not allowed. He spotted a teacher and clutching his leg

◇ ◆ ◇ ◆ ◇ ◆ ◇ ◆ ◇ ◆ ◇ ◆ ◇ ◆ ◇ ◆ ◇ ◆ ◇ ◆ ◇ ◆ ◇ ◆ ◇ ◆ ◇ ◆ ◇ ◆ ◇ ◆ ◇ ◆

PHOTOCOPIABLE PAGE

◆ Ben's story ◆

he cried at the top of his voice, "She just ran into me and knocked me over." The teacher sent Ben off to the first aid room. Ben limped his way through the hall stopping to look over his shoulder at the little girl, who was now crying as the teacher shouted at her for running in school.

Ben looked at the clock. Was there really another half hour to go before lunch time? He looked at his work book and put up his hand, "Can I go to the toilet please? I don't feel very well."

His teacher looked up from the group she was working with and went over to him. Ben began to clutch his tummy and made a funny croaking sound in his throat. He was ushered from the classroom by a now anxious teacher uttering soothing comments. "Never mind, Ben, I am sure you will feel better soon. You have a little lie down and see how you feel in a while."

Ben smiled. This was much better than writing the story he had left behind in the classroom. At five to twelve Ben sat up. He had enjoyed his little rest, but he was beginning to feel rather hungry and he had a football match to play. He went back into the classroom and told his teacher that he felt much better. He went to his desk and picked up his pencil just as the bell went.

Ben had been told to go home straight after school. His mum wanted him to go shopping with her. Ben loathed shopping. He walked home very slowly taking the longest route. As he turned the corner his mum was on the doorstep. "Where have you been? You know very well I wanted to go shopping."

Ben looked up and smiled. He put on his sweetest, how to get round Mum, voice. "It's not my fault. I really wanted to come, but there was an accident and the police wouldn't let me cross the road. It was horrible." He put up his arm and began to wipe pretend tears from his eyes. Mum put her arm around his shoulders and steered him inside.

"You go and put the television on, love, and I will bring you a drink and something to eat. It must have been a terrible shock for you. Now never mind about the shopping. I can go later on my own when Dad gets home."

Ben spent the rest of the evening doing what he liked best, watching television and eating sweets, crisps and biscuits.

◆ The bully ◆

You know it's quite a mystery

why Glenford likes to bully me

when I've done nothing at all

he pushes me and then I fall.

At playtime sitting on the benches

he showers me with spiteful punches.

Teacher, teacher can't you see

How Glenford Lewis bullies me?

He says that if I ever tell

both my cheeks are sure to swell.

Things could not get much worse

so I think I'll tell my parents first.

Pauline Stewart

PHOTOCOPIABLE PAGE

◆ Left out ◆

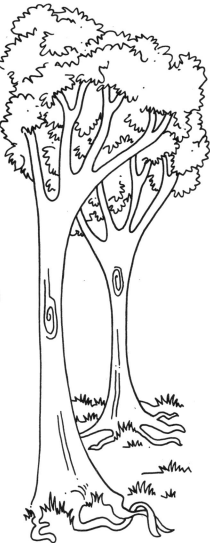

It feels as if pins

Are pricking my eyes.

My face is burning hot.

A firework is trying

To go off inside me.

My feet are glued to the spot.

My hands are rocks in my pockets

I want to run away.

But my legs are rooted to the ground

Like trees. I have to stay

And listen

To everyone calling me names

And not letting me

Join in with their games.

Celia Warren

◆ The playground ◆

PHOTOCOPIABLE PAGE

Hopscotch ◆ Me as a citizen

◆ Vote for me ◆

People with blonde hair will be in charge of keeping our towns and cities clean.

People with blue eyes will pay no more tax and get the best jobs.

Vote for me because…

There will be free bicycles for the under fives and over seventies.

Parks and playing fields will be turned into car parks.

Recycling is an expensive waste of money. It must be stopped now!

No-one uses buses anymore so, to make money, I will treble bus fares.

Children will be made to finish all incomplete school work on Saturday mornings.

◆ Vote for me ◆

People who drop litter and damage the environment will be fined.

Bus fares will be reduced to encourage more people to use the buses.

Secure bike sheds will be provided for all schools.

Vote for me because…

Bike routes will be developed along all roads leading to schools.

Community youth centres will be set up in all areas.

School playing fields and swimming pools will be opened to the public at weekends.

As part of the school curriculum, all children will be given road safety lessons and taught how to ride a bike.

PHOTOCOPIABLE PAGE